THE HOW AND WHY WONDER BOOK OF
EXTINCT ANIMALS

Written by JOHN BURTON
Illustrated by JOHN BARBER

GROSSET & DUNLAP • Publishers • NEW YORK

Introduction

Animals are constantly evolving. Just as new ones appear, so others disappear. Some, like crocodiles, remain unchanged for millions of years, while others evolve rapidly. Man evolved fairly recently, and in the last few hundred years he has spread out over the whole world. In doing so, he has killed countless millions of animals, some for food, some because they were pests, and some for "sport."

Man has also wiped out entire species. Once a species is extinct, it can never be resurrected, however much we regret its passing.

Fortunately, more and more people are becoming aware of this and are trying to stop the destruction of wildlife. Societies like the World Wildlife Fund buy reservations where animals can live in peace. Governments protect animals so that their people can enjoy seeing them; wild animals are for *everyone,* not for merely a few hunters.

A few wealthy ladies wearing leopard-skin coats could deprive children living in the year 2000 of the opportunity to see a live leopard. If we want to continue to see leopards, tigers, pandas, crocodiles, and other animals, we must make sure that they do not become extinct.

Library of Congress Catalog Card Number 74-418

ISBN: 0-448-05072-2 (Wonder Book Edition)
ISBN: 0-448-04062-X (Trade Edition)
ISBN: 0-448-03866-8 (Library Edition)

Published in the United States by
Grosset & Dunlap, Inc., New York, N.Y.

FIRST PRINTING 1975

Originally published in Great Britain
by Transworld Publishers Ltd.
Transworld Edition published 1972.
Copyright © 1972 Transworld Publishers Ltd.

CONTENTS

If we think of the world as having been created in seven days, then life as we know it has existed for a brief time. On the last day of the week life appeared, and just before midnight man appeared.

Extinct Animals Long Ago
and Their Fossil Remains

How do we know about extinct animals?
Some of the animals that are extinct now have died out only recently, and so there may be photographs and detailed descriptions of these animals, as well as stuffed specimens in museums. Animals that have become extinct as recently as this include the *quagga* (a relative of the zebra) and the passenger pigeon.

Ancient rock-paintings, such as the Stone Age paintings in the caves at Lascaux in France, or Altamira in Spain, also give a good idea of the animals found 20,000 years ago or more.

4

But most of the extinct animals died out millions of years ago, long before there were any people to paint them or write about them. How, then, do we know about all these animals? From fossils.

Fossils are the remains of animals and **What are fossils?** plants that have been preserved in the ground, often quite literally "turned to stone." When an animal dies, its remains are usually eaten by other animals. Even the bones are often crunched by scavengers such as hyenas. Sometimes, however, bits of the animal, usually the bones, but sometimes the whole animal, are buried. Normally, the re-

mains continue to decompose slowly, even after they have become buried. Sometimes, however, the animal is buried quickly. This usually happens in rivers, ponds, marshes, and estuaries, where the dead animal sinks rapidly into the oozy mud, and is sealed off from air and its effects. Sometimes only impressions of animals are preserved — these are also called fossils — but sometimes bones are preserved also.

Fossils are studied by paleontologists (from the Greek *palaios*, meaning ancient, and *logia*, meaning study or knowledge of). When fossils are found, they are usually transported to a museum with much of the surrounding

When an animal dies, its bones are sometimes preserved as a fossil.

A paleontologist using a dental drill to carefully clean a fossil.

rock and often a protective casing of plaster of Paris. The paleontologist slowly and carefully removes the fossil from the casing and rock. He uses many different tools, such as hammers and chisels, to remove the larger pieces of rock; a dentists' drill and acids get the finer details to stand out.

Geological time is the length of time

What is geological time?

that the earth has been in existence. Geologists divide it into periods, or epochs, each of which usually lasted several millions of years. They are known by names such as Jurassic, Cretaceous, Eocene, and Pleistocene. History started only about 5,000 years ago, but the Pleistocene Epoch (the last major geological period) started about three and a half million years ago. To a paleontologist, three and a half million years is very recent, indeed — the fossils he may be studying from the Triassic Period are over 220 million years old!

When fossils were first found, no one

When fossils were first found, what did people think they were?

really knew what they were. Various ideas were suggested as to how the fishes and shells managed to get to the top of mountains. The most popularly believed idea was that they were animals that failed to get into Noah's ark, and were drowned when the flood came. These creatures were referred to as *antediluvial* — that is to say, before (*ante*) the flood (*diluvial*). Most people believed implicitly in the Bible, and it was heretical to suggest other ways that the animals may have arrived at the tops of mountains. Scientists began studying the fossils more and more carefully and realized that most of the animals no longer existed — so the idea was advanced that there had been several creations. The studies continued, and in 1831 a young man named

Charles Darwin set off on a round-the-world voyage as the resident naturalist on HMS *Beagle*. An extremely acute observer, he made a collection of fossils while he was in South America. For years afterwards, he thought about all the animals he had seen on his voyage — both living animals and extinct fossilized animals — and he gradually worked out one of the most revolutionary theories of the century. In 1859 he published a book, *The Origin of the Species,* in which he explained how species are constantly evolving, with some becoming extinct. He also concluded that this took not just a few hundred years, but millions and millions of years.

Charles Darwin collected many fossils in South America. He noticed that many of them were similar to living animals.

APATOSAURUS

IGUANODON

STEGOSAURUS

During the Cretaceous era, dinosaurs were the dominant inhabitants of the earth.

What were dinosaurs? When the dinosaurs were first discovered, early in the nineteenth century, it was not realized exactly what they were. The first one described was *Megalosaurus* (which simply means "big lizard"). It was described by Dean William Buckland, an eccentric geologist and clergyman who lived in Oxford. The next dinosaur to be recognized was *Iguanodon* (iguana-tooth), discovered by a Sussex doctor and geologist, Gideon Mantell. But it was Sir Richard Owen, superintendent of the Natural History Department of the British Museum, who, in 1841, coined the word *dinosaur* to describe these giant reptiles.

Dinosaur derived from two Greek words: *deinos,* meaning terrible; and *sauros,* meaning reptile or lizard.

It was in the United States, however, that the greatest finds of dinosaurs were to be made, precipitating a famous and bitter feud. The rivals were Othniel Marsh, professor of paleontology at Yale University, and Edward Drinker Cope, from Philadelphia. The famous "Battle of the Bones" really began in 1877. The two scientists accused each other of all sorts of things — even of destroying bones so that the other would not be able to get any. They were both very wealthy men when the feud started, but they both spent enormous fortunes

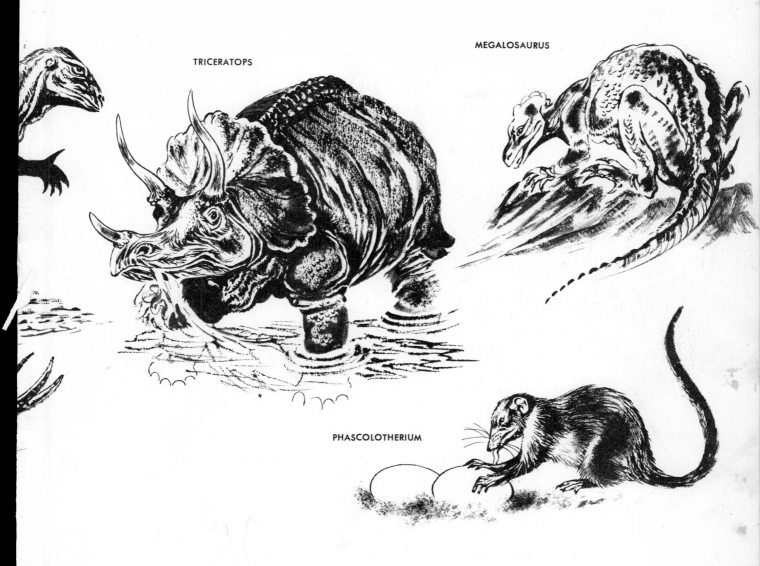

TRICERATOPS

MEGALOSAURUS

PHASCOLOTHERIUM

in their search for dinosaur bones. Between them, they were the discoverers of many well-known dinosaurs: *Apatosaurus, Stegosaurus, Triceratops,* and *Camarasaurus.*

From the Triassic Period and during the Cretaceous Period, until about 70 million years ago, dinosaurs were commonplace all over the wrold.

The Cretaceous Period did not suddenly come to an end — there were changes, but they took hundreds, or even thousands, of years. Dinosaurs did not become extinct overnight, but gradually died out over thousands of years as vegetation and climate were altered.

Some animals have survived from the Age of Reptiles almost unchanged — the so-called "living fossils." When an animal is described as a "living fossil," what is really meant is that it has hardly changed in appearance from its fossil ancestors. The tuatara, which is found in New Zealand, is a good example. Fossil tuataras have been found in Jurassic strata that are almost identical to the one still found on small islands near New Zealand. The crocodiles alive today, as well as the turtles, have also remained almost unchanged. Many of the species alive today look like those that inhabited the earth at the time of the dinosaurs.

WOOLLY RHINO

REINDEER

Thousands of years ago, London had an arctic climate. Mammoths, reindeer, and woolly rhinos lived there.

The Ice Age

What was the Ice Age?

Geologists divide time into different periods — each of which lasts several millions of years. The different periods have become famous for particular reasons — the Cretaceous Period, for instance, is often referred to as the Age of Reptiles, because at that time the giant reptiles, the dinosaurs, were commonplace. The most recent period is referred to by geologists as the Pleistocene, or the Ice Age, a time when much of Europe was intermittently covered by sheets of ice. The climate was quite different during the periods when the snow and ice covered North America and parts of Europe — these periods were known as glacial periods, when the climate was like that found in Greenland today. But then there were periods of warmer weather, known as the interglacial periods, when the climate was similar to that of East Africa today. These changes took place over thousands of years — in fact, geologists do not really know whether or not the Ice Age has finished. It is possible that we are living in one of the warmer interglacial periods, and that in about 10,000 years' time most of North America will be covered with snow and ice once more.

Dragons' teeth were the teeth of extinct animals found by the Chinese in caves. In 1870 the superintendent of natural history at the British Museum, Sir Richard Owen, wrote an article on the fossil animals of China, and based it mainly on specimens that had been bought in druggists' shops in the Far East as charms. The animals included rhinoceroses, orangutans, giant pandas, pigs, buffaloes, and even three-toed horses.

What are dragons' teeth and how do they tell us about the Ice Age?

When foundations are dug for new buildings, fossils are likely to be found. The fossils found in London show that it was a very different place in the past.

Fossils have shown that during one of the glacial, or icy, periods, when London must have looked like arctic Scandinavia or Alaska, there were cave bears, wolves, red deer, woolly mammoths, reindeer, polar bears, and giant beavers. During one of the warmer spells, it was more like East Africa of today. There were bison, hippos, hyenas, cave lions, boar, and straight-tusked elephants.

STRAIGHT-TUSKED ELEPHANT

CAVE LION

HIPPO

HYENA

In the warmer periods of the Ice Age animals similar to those now found in Africa might have been seen in the Thames River—hippos, cave lions, hyenas, and straight-tusked elephants.

Frozen mammoth meat, when first found, was so fresh that it was fed to dogs.

Every now and then, the tribesmen living in Siberia would find a frozen mammoth buried in the ice. They believed that the mammoths were a kind of giant mole and that they died when they saw the light of day. This was because the mammoth started to decompose as soon as it began to thaw. The tribesmen who found the mammoths would sell the ivory of the tusks and feed the meat to their dogs. The ivory was sold to merchants, and eventually some of it found its way to western Europe. In 1806, an English scientist organized an expedition to Siberia and managed to bring back some bones and some pieces of skin, which are now preserved in the Natural History Museum in Leningrad.

Have frozen animals ever been found?

Mammoths had long woolly coats that kept out the cold, but they were such large, heavy animals, that if they fell into a crevice in the ice or frozen ground, they were unable to climb out and soon froze to death. Over 100,000 mammoth tusks and many bones have now been found in the frozen ground.

One of the best preserved mammoths was found by scientists sent out by the Academy of Sciences in St. Petersburg (now Leningrad) in 1901. At Beresovka, in northern Siberia, they found a woolly mammoth so well preserved that it even had the remains of food in its stomach, and they were able to examine the blood from its veins. The plants on which it had been feeding were mainly grasses, but also some buttercups. By using modern ways of determining dates (carbon-14 tests), it was found that this mammoth died about 44,000 years ago.

Early man probably hunted mammoths, but it is unlikely that he caused their extinction. Cave paintings and pieces of ivory with carvings of mammoths on them have been found at several places.

Woolly rhinos have also been found in the icy wastes of Siberia. Like the mammoths, they had long shaggy coats to keep out the cold, but quickly froze to death when trapped in icy ground.

One of the best preserved woolly rhinoceroses was found not in ice, but in a mixture of oil and salts, at Starunia, in the eastern Carpathian Mountains of Poland. Only the hoofs and tusks had disappeared.

How do we know which wild animals cave men hunted?

Early men sometimes used caves for shelter, and occasionally they painted pictures on the walls, usually of the animals they hunted. The most famous of these caves are the ones at Lascaux, France, containing pictures of bison, wild horses, reindeer, mammoths, and wild cattle. None of these animals live in the area of the caves any more. Early men also shared their caves with animals such as cave lions and cave bears. The story of the extinction of the cave bear is a very strange one, indeed.

The Ice Age was interrupted by periods of warmer weather, during which many animals we think of as being typically African lived as far north as Durham, England, including hippos and

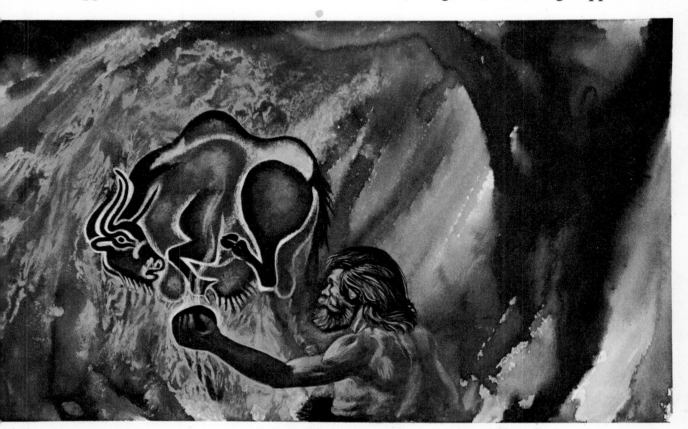

Stone Age men painted pictures of the animals that once roamed Europe.

Primitive man hunted the enormous cave bears. They also collected their skulls.

elephants. It was during these warm spells — or interglacial periods — that the cave bear, feeding on abundant fruit and vegetables, gradually evolved into a giant of an animal. It sometimes reached twelve feet and of course it had hardly any enemies. Hundreds of thousands of years later, the weather gradually became colder again. Snow and ice once more spread across Europe. The elephants and hippos moved south or died out, but the cave bear spent the long cold winter hibernating in caves. The winters got longer and longer. Many bears died of starvation, and many of those that survived got dis-

eases through not having enough exercise and being starved. While sealed in their caves, they lived on body fat accumulated during the summer.

Cave bears also had another enemy, Neanderthal man, a cave man closely related to ourselves but who was not quite so intelligent. These cave men used to hunt the bears—probably by filling the caves with smoke, blinding them with flaming torches, and then clubbing them to death. Hundreds of skulls and other

Did men eat cave bears and other cave-dwelling animals?

bones of cave bears have been found in some caves, all stacked up in neat piles. These may have been animals killed as sacrifices.

In caves in South America the remains of another completely different animal have been found. These were giant sloths. Unlike their living relatives, the giant sloths could not climb trees. They used their massive hind-quarters to anchor their bodies while they pulled trees over to browse on the leaves. When the first Indians arrived in South America, they probably hunted giant sloths — but the animals were already on the way to extinction.

The South American Indians may well have hunted elephants! When the Mongol ancestors of the Indians crossed from Asia into Alaska, there were mammoths in the northern regions, and the colonists of South America probably hunted mastodons several hundred years later.

Pieces of skin of the extinct giant sloth have been found in South American caves.

The tar pit of Rancho La Brea in California has provided one of the biggest collections of fossils ever found in one spot. At Rancho La Brea, tar seeped through the earth's surface, forming pools.

Which animals have been found in tar pits?

Small animals would probably be able to run across the sticky surface of the tar without too much difficulty, and they would probably be attracted by pools of water that collected on the surface. But any large animal attempting to venture onto the tar soon became trapped. The struggles of the dying animals attracted meat-eating animals and scavengers, who would also get caught. The corpses soon sank into the tar, where some of the most complete and best preserved fossils have been found.

The species found in the Rancho La Brea tar pit include extinct species of mice, coyotes, eagles, owls, condors, puma, bears, bison, camels, peccaries, and many others. Two of the most famous animals found there were the dire wolf and the saber-toothed cat (often called the saber-toothed tiger). These predators were attracted to the tar pit by the animals trapped there, only to die themselves.

Some of the best preserved fossils in the world are those of animals trapped in tar pits.

CONDOR

SABER-TOOTHED TIGER

BISON

Once slaughtered by the thousands, the passenger pigeon is now extinct.

Man Spreads Over the World
—and the Animals Disappear

The most common bird to have been exterminated by man was undoubtedly the passenger

What was the most common bird to have become extinct?

pigeon of North America. In fact, the passenger pigeon may once have been the most common bird in the world. Some of the flocks were simply enormous. The famous ornithologist Alexander Wilson described a flock that "darkened the sky" — it was several miles across and took hours to pass overhead. He calculated the size of the flock — using the time it took to pass over, its width, and the number of birds

passing over per minute — and estimated there were over two billion birds in this one flock. He reckoned there were 2,230,272,000 birds. This was in 1810; by 1900 they were practically extinct. About a hundred years ago a nesting colony 28 miles long and between three and four miles wide was seen in Michigan. But, as the railways spread, so did the rate at which man destroyed the passenger pigeon. Enormous numbers were slaughtered, mainly for food — one depot in New York handled about 18,000 birds a day in 1855. By 1879 something like 5,000 men worked full time as passenger pig-

The extinct great auk of the North Atlantic was flightless like the penguins of the Antarctic; so was the dodo. Both were easy prey for man and his animals.

eon hunters—and hundreds more local hunters would join in. In 1879 about one billion birds were killed in Michigan alone!

Not only did the passenger pigeon migrate in vast flocks, but as already mentioned, it nested in huge colonies. It was possibly this habit that led in part to its rapid extinction. Many birds nest in dense colonies — the predators cannot kill enough to make much difference to the overall success of the colony — but when man comes on the scene, he really can make a difference with his super-efficient ways of killing. Once the flocks were reduced to less than a cer-

tain number, they were doomed. The last nest was found in 1894.

Passenger pigeons had been bred on many occasions in zoos and in private aviaries — but everything about their extinction happened rapidly, before anyone seemed really aware of what was going on. The last passenger pigeon in the world, "Martha," died on September 1, 1914, in the Cincinnati Zoo. Plenty of passenger pigeons were stuffed — they are pretty birds — and they are still on display in most of the larger natural history museums of the world, but no one will ever see passenger pigeons flying in the wild again.

The great auk was once found in many

What happened to the great auk?

parts of the North Atlantic Ocean, including Britain and North America. It was related to the razorbills, guillemots, puffins, and murres, but it was much larger, standing about two and a half feet high. Its wings were small and useless for flight. In fact, it looked very much like the penguins which are found in the Southern Hemisphere. Sailors from Scandinavia, and the islanders living in the Faeroes, the Hebrides, the Shetlands, the Orkneys, and Iceland, all hunted the great auk, as well as many other species of seabird. The Eskimos and other inhabitants of North America also hunted them. It was probably because they were flightless and unable to nest in particularly inaccessible places that they were easy to catch, and by the beginning of the nineteenth century they were well on the way to extinction. The last few eggs were eagerly hunted by collectors. In June, 1844, the last pair of auks was killed near Iceland. Odd auks were seen from time to time for a few years afterwards, but all that is known of the great auk today are a few skins and eggs in museums — though, two hundred years ago, they were still being harvested for food.

The term, "as dead as a dodo," has

What does "as dead as a dodo" mean?

come to be used to describe anything that is extinct — and cannot be made to come back. The dodos were strange birds found only on islands in the Indian Ocean. The best-known dodo is the one once found on the island of Mauritius. This dodo became extinct about 1680.

Sailors from passing ships killed the dodos, which were very easy to catch, for food; but is was probably the pigs that were allowed to run loose all over the island which finally exterminated the dodo. The dodo was flightless and built its nest on the ground, and the eggs provided an attractive source of food for the semi-wild pigs.

The dodo was a very strange-looking bird: it had a bulky body with a massive head and beak, and large, strong feet. The wings were ridiculous, useless little sprouts, and the tail looked as if it had been added as an afterthought.

Moas looked like ostriches. The Maoris hunted some species, but now they are all extinct.

New Zealand was originally uninhabited by mammals, except for two species of bats. All the other mammals came with the human colonists, first with the Maoris and then with the Europeans. The vegetation was rich, lush and extremely varied, so the birds developed into types quite distinct from those found anywhere else in the world. In the grassy plains, where deer or antelope would have been found in other parts of the world, there were large flightless birds resembling ostriches. These were the moas. There were about twenty different species of moa; some were large, standing nearly

Did flightless birds become extinct on larger islands?

twelve feet tall, others were no larger than a chicken. They were found mainly in the grassy plains (and known as lawn-moas!)

When the Polynesians first colonized New Zealand around A.D. 950 there were still many species of moa found there, though they were probably already declining. The vegetation of New Zealand was changing to a more forested type, and as the grassy plains disappeared, so would the moas. The Maoris, who arrived in the fourteenth century, hunted many species of moa and no doubt helped them on their way to extinction — some are known for certain to have been hunted by the Maoris. Four species probably survived into the fifteenth century, and one still survived as late as 1785. Archaeologists have found the remains of moas in the kitchen refuse of Maori campsites, including bits of feathers and parts of eggs.

The huia, of New Zealand, is quite unrelated to the moa, but also extinct. It was a forest-dwelling bird, found deep in undisturbed forests. Male and female huias had a working partnership — no other birds are known to have helped each other as they did. The male had a short chisel-shaped bill with which he hammered away at rotting tree trunks to expose insects and grubs. The female had a long, slender, curved bill with which she extracted the grubs for herself and her mate. The clearing of New Zealand's forests soon destroyed suitable trees, and the last reliable observation of a huia was in 1907.

Did large birds live anywhere else in the world?

Giant birds have been evident in several parts of the world. Most of them died out before man appeared. The giant elephant bird of Madagascar, however, probably lived on into historic times. It is thought, in fact, that stories of this bird told by traders and merchants probably started the legend of the roc — the mythical bird that Sinbad the Sailor encountered. The enormous eggs of these now-extinct birds can still be found in Madagascar, though they are usually broken. It is easy to believe the stories of a bird that fed on elephants — a bird laying such large eggs must surely have been of gigantic proportions. The egg of an elephant bird was about three feet in circumference and held more than two gallons of fluid.

The giant eggs of the elephant bird gave rise to the legend of the roc, which carried off Sinbad.

NENÉ

HONEY CREEPER

In the past 200 years, more birds have become extinct in Hawaii than anywhere else in the world.

Many of the birds that have become extinct, or are very rare, are flightless. They

Why is it that some birds cannot fly?

also often lived on islands. When these birds first colonized the islands, there were few other birds or animals, and so they were not hunted. They rarely needed to fly to escape. Also, on a fairly small island, there is always the risk that during a storm a bird in flight will be blown out to sea — so it could be a real advantage to be unable to fly.

Throughout the thousands of years since they first colonized the islands, many of the birds had lost their power of flight. They were at a real disadvan-

tage when man came along. Not only did man hunt many of the birds for food, but he also brought with him many other animals which were released on the islands. The rats, pigs, goats, dogs, cats, and mongooses which men introduced all over the world destroyed the natural vegetation or preyed on the eggs of ground-nesting birds. Many of the flightless birds found on islands were found nowhere else in the world — some fifteen species of rails (wading birds) have become extinct in the last three hundred years or so. Most of these rails were flightless, and their extinction was caused by man's arrival on the islands.

Captain Cook was presented with a beautiful feather cloak in Hawaii.

The Hawaiian Islands were once inhabited by a dazzling array of beautiful birds. Some are still to be found there, but many of them have died out. The Polynesians who were living in the Hawaiian Islands when Captain Cook arrived had not had much effect on the wildlife — but the European, and later the American, settlers started chopping down the forests and brought with them rats, pigs, and lots of different sorts of birds, from all over the world. Of the sixty-eight different species of birds once found on the Hawaiian Islands, forty of them are probably extinct now.

Why have so many birds become extinct on the Hawaiian Islands?

Many of the birds were beautiful, and their skins were used by the Hawaiians to make robes and ornaments for important occasions. At one time they were blamed for the extinction of several of the birds, but it is obvious now that they had very little to do with it. When Captain James Cook visited Hawaii, he was presented with some beautiful feather capes. These were made from red and yellow feathers, but when mohos, which had tufts of yellow feathers on their shoulders, became rare, and yellow feathers difficult to obtain, they used black feathers as well. Many of the birds are known by their beautiful, and unusual Hawaiian names: *o-o, mamo, ou, palila, ula-ai-hawane, akialoa, nukupuu.*

Steller's sea cow was extinct 27 years after it was discovered.

Steller's sea cow was a large ungainly

Which animal disappeared the fastest? sea mammal related to the dugongs and the manatees. These animals, peering out of the sea, and covered with seaweed, are supposed to have given rise to stories about mermaids! Scientists gave this order of water mammals the name Sirenia — after the mythical sirens who lured sailors to their doom.

Steller's sea cow was the largest of the "sirens," growing to over twenty-five feet in length. It was a sluggish animal that fed on underwater plants. When it was discovered in 1741, it was already fairly uncommon. Whaling parties easily slaughtered the defenseless, slow-moving, somewhat dull-witted animal, and by 1768 (only twenty-seven years after they had been discovered) they were probably extinct.

All that remain now are a few skeletons in museums and traveler's descriptions.

During the Ice Age, lions were found

Have lions ever been found in Europe? as far north as Britain, occurring throughout Europe, through France, Holland, Germany, Austria, Switzerland, and also as far away as Siberia. These lions were known as cave lions, and may have been slightly different in appearance from modern lions. In Greece there were still lions in historical times. When Xerxes was attempting to conquer Greece in 480 B.C., his equipment carriers were attacked by lions in Macedonia in northern Greece. Aristotle, who wrote the first real natural history book, noted that lions were rare in Greece (this was in about 300 B.C.).

In 480 BC Xerxes' equipment carriers were attacked by lions, in Greece.

In the first century another writer recorded that the lions that were once found in Macedonia were extinct.

Lions were also very common in many parts of North Africa and the Middle East. Nearly all the ancient civilizations portrayed their kings hunting lions. The tombs of the Pharaohs of Egypt and the kings of Babylon and other famous states include many sculptures and paintings of lion hunts. At the time of the Crusades there were still lions in the Holy Land — the descendants of the lions known to Samson. Now the only place where any number survive outside Africa is the forest of Gir in India. If that forest can be protected, there is no reason why the lion population should not increase.

Which horses have become extinct? In prehistoric times, horses and their relatives were widespread in Europe, Asia, and Africa. As man spread, he also domesticated one of the wild horses. As land was turned into farmland and plowed or grazed, the wild horses became a nuisance, and so they were hunted. The wild horses and their relatives comprise two horses, several wild asses, the donkey, and several zebras. Many of these have disappeared or are extremely rare. Two Asiatic horses were once widespread, but the small tarpan was hunted to extinction in the 1880's, and Przewalski's horse has almost died out in the wild — though a few are kept in zoos.

The Pharaohs were often portrayed hunting lions.

The other type of horse to become extinct in recent times is the quagga. It was striped like a zebra on the forequarters and plain like a horse on the hindquarters. When the first settlers arrived in South Africa, they roamed the plains in large herds. But the quagga, unfortunately, along with other zebra and antelope, ate the same food as the cattle the settlers brought with them, and so the farmers set about exterminating wildlife. They were successful. The only place the quagga can be seen now is in museums or in photographs.

Wild horses are among the animals man has made rare or extinct. The tarpan and the quagga both become extinct in the nineteenth century. Przewalski's horse is now found mainly in zoos.

TARPAN

QUAGGA

PRZEWALSKI'S HORSE

When Europeans discovered Australia, they were amazed at the animals to be seen. Most of the mammals were marsupials — animals that carry their young in pouches. Safe in Australia, these primitive mammals had survived millions of years. When the Europeans arrived, about eight different species were to become extinct and many more were to become extremely rare.

Which marsupials have vanished?

The marsupials are extremely variable — there are grazing marsupials, such as the kangaroos, burrowing mole-like marsupials, mouse-like, shrew-like, and even flesh-eating species. The largest of the flesh-eaters is the thylacine, or Tasmanian wolf.

The thylacine is now on the verge of extinction. Every few years this animal is sighted, and in 1966 the Australian government set aside 1,600,000 acres as a reservation, in which it was hoped that most of the surviving thylacines lived. This same government had, around 1900, paid a bounty for every thylacine killed. The thylacine is dog-like in appearance, but with a long thin tail and dark stripes on its back. It was shot, poisoned and trapped by farmers for stealing chickens and killing sheep.

Over twenty-five different marsupials are in serious danger of becoming extinct. Even now, although it is against the law to export any live Australian animals without a permit, it is a common sight to see remote areas littered with the corpses of kangaroos.

Within historical times, several animals have become extinct in what is now Great Britain. Until well into the Middle Ages (and much later in many parts of the country), many of the forests of England were inhabited by wolves. Wolves, in fact, survived until the eighteenth century — the last

What animals became extinct in Great Britain?

one is believed to have been killed in Sutherland in 1743.

The brown bear became extinct much earlier, though no one knows for certain exactly when it died out. It probably survived until the eleventh century in Scotland. Being much more remote and with a very much smaller population, Scotland was the last stronghold of several animals that have now disappeared. The reindeer was described by Norwegian visitors to Caithness in the twelfth century. They have since died out, but then, a few years ago, a herd was reintroduced into the Cairngorms. The capercaillie, a large forest-dwelling gamebird which also eventually became extinct, even in Scotland, was also reintroduced and now flourishes once more. Wildcats and pine martens were both more or less exterminated over most of their range in Great Britain, but have managed to survive in remote parts of Scotland.

KANGAROO

PINE MARTEN

THYLACINE

REINDEER

At one time bison were found over a vast area and slaughtered. They were just barely saved from extinction.

The Effort to Save Animals

Many animals are on the verge of extinction today.

What are the causes of animal extinction?

There are many reasons why this is so, and there are usually reasons why a particular animal is in danger. Some animals have decreased in number for hundreds of years due to changes in climate and vegetation. For instance, the giant panda and the whooping crane are both rare, probably for these reasons. Other animals, such as the North American bison and the Arabian oryx, are rare because of senseless and destructive hunting. But probably most endangered animals are threatened because of man's intrusion in the places in which they live.

When the first settlers were moving across America's "Wild West," the herds of bison (or buffalo, as

How many buffalo were there in America?

they are sometimes called) seemed limitless. There were probably sixty million bison roaming the plains in herds that often contained several thousand animals. As the settlers spread across the prairies, so the hunters went ahead. Sometimes they were employed to supply meat for workmen on the railroads, but often the slaughter was far greater than was needed to supply their needs. At that time it seemed that the bison would last forever — but by the beginning of this century there were only a

few hundred left throughout America. By careful conservation, man has now managed to re-establish several large herds, and in the National Parks of Canada and the U.S.A. these magnificent animals can once more be seen.

Few people realize that a bison very similar to the one found in America once roamed Europe. The European bison, or wisent, lived mainly in deep forests. As the forests were cut down, so the bison were hunted and exterminated. By the beginning of the twentieth century, they existed only deep in the forest of Bialowieza, in Poland. They were fairly safe there until World War I, when a shortage of food led to the slaughter of the last 737. Luckily, there were several zoos, and after the war as many as possible were gathered together in an enclosure in the Bialowieza Forest and allowed to breed. In 1956 some were allowed to roam wild, and since then small herds have been released in remote forests in Russia and Romania. There are also small herds of bison in several zoos.

What other large animals are in danger?

There are five living species of rhinoceroses which could become extinct in the near future. Two species are so close to it that it is unlikely that anything will be done in time to save them. The five species are the black and the white rhinoceroses of Africa, and the Indian, Sumatran, and Javan rhinoceroses of Asia.

The most numerous species is the black rhino, though even this species is decreasing very quickly. Black rhinos once roamed the plains of Africa by the thousands, but now they have been exterminated over most of their former range. The white rhino has suffered even more — its name comes not from its color, but from a mispronunciation of the Afrikaans name, wide (wijd)-lipped rhino. After the elephants, the white rhino is the largest living land mammal. A large male can be up to six and a half feet tall at the shoulder and weigh over three tons. In recent years it has increased its numbers in some parts of its range and attempts are being made to breed it in captivity.

The rhinos of Asia, on the other hand, are in a really serious situation. The great Indian rhino is a large species standing over six feet tall, and looks almost armor-plated. At one time it was found in many parts of northern India and Nepal (it is a water-loving species,

JAVAN RHINO

SUMATRAN RHINO

In Asia, rhinos are killed for their horn. The Javan and the Sumatran rhinos are on the verge of extinction.

and rarely found very far from a wallow). Although sanctuaries have been set up for the protection of the rhinos, there is still considerable poaching. The poachers want only the horn which is widely believed by the Chinese and other Orientals to have medicinal properties. Considerable sums of money are paid for the horns.

The Javan rhino was, until about a century ago, quite widely distributed. It was found in most of Southeast Asia as far as the Chinese border, and at the beginning of this century was still being hunted around Saigon. It was also once found on Sumatra, but the last ones died just before the Second World War. It is now one of the rarest animals in the world — there may be as few as twenty-

five left in the wild. A reservation has been set aside to protect them and also the few remaining Javan tigers, which are the rarest carnivores in the world. It seems unlikely that the Javan rhinos can survive without more protection.

The Sumatran rhino is small and somewhat hairy. It is not confined to the island of Sumatra. It is found also on Borneo, in Burma, Malaya, and perhaps in adjacent countries. Altogether it is doubtful if there are more than two hundred left in the wild — in fact, it is quite likely that there are less than a hundred of them left alive. Most of them are in a reservation on Sumatra, and if they can be guarded against poachers, there is a chance that their numbers might increase.

The Arabian oryx has become very well known through the efforts of naturalists to preserve it from what was very nearly certain extinction. It was once found over a large part of Arabia and the Middle East, and was fairly common. It was safe from hunters, it was able to live under the extremely harsh conditions of the desert, it was very fast, and it could travel over long distances without water. From a distance it looked like a white horse with a single long curved horn. Oryxes seen in the distance may have given rise to the descriptions of the mythical unicorn.

Is there any hope that the Arabian oryx will survive?

With the development of the oil industry in the Middle East, wealthy oil sheiks began hunting the oryx with modern automatic weapons from fast-moving jeeps and cars. The oryxes did not have a chance, and they were soon exterminated over large parts of their range. They are now reduced to only a few hundred, at the most, in the wild. Fortunately, however, some have been captured and small breeding herds have been started in captivity — some in Arabia and one in Arizona. At least the species is fairly safe from extermination, and perhaps one day oryxes will roam the Arabian deserts again safely.

Rich oil sheiks helped to exterminate the oryx, hunting from cars with automatic weapons.

The story of the whooping crane is un-

Has the whooping crane been saved?

finished. So far it has hovered on the brink of disaster for several years — but it will be a few years before anyone can say for certain that they are safe. The whooping crane has probably been fairly rare for some considerable time — even before man's interference. It is thought that in 1870 there were only 1,300 birds; unfortunately, by 1942, this number has decreased to only 23. They were strictly protected by then, but no one knew where they nested — the last nest had been found in 1922.

They were seen only in migration and on their wintering grounds at the now-famous Aransas Refuge in Texas. Then, in 1955, a bird sitting on its nest was spotted from an airplane. The nest was in the vast Wood Buffalo Park in Canada, a National Park of nearly 11 million acres. By careful surveillance, both from land and from the air, more nests were located. A careful check is kept on them. The annual "census" is taken when the birds arrive at Aransas. Despite bad years when few, or even no, young have been raised, there has been a steady increase over the years and there are now about 50 birds.

The whooping crane nests in remote parts of Wood Buffalo Park in Canada.

The giant panda is used as a symbol for conservationists.

The giant panda has become famous as the animal chosen by the World Wildlife Fund as its symbol. The first live panda to be seen outside China was the one shown in the Chicago zoo in 1936. This, and other pandas shown in zoos elsewhere, were very popular with the public, and pandas have remained a firm favorite. The home of the panda is in remote bamboo forests in China. A panda looks like a black and white bear.

Where is the giant panda found?

Although known to be quite rare, they have never been hunted a great deal, except for a period during the 1930's, when many were shot or captured for museums and zoos. Their number is not very large, as they are found only in the remote bamboo jungles of Szechwan — but so long as these jungles are left intact, the giant panda should be safe. In recent years, several have been bred in Chinese zoos. They are completely protected by the Chinese government.

The largest animals the world has ever known have been brought to the verge of extinction by man's greed.

Whales are the largest animals that have ever lived — even the largest of the tremendous dinosaurs is believed to have weighed only about 50 tons! The blue whale may weigh over 150 tons and grow to nearly 100 feet in length. Even its new-born babies are bigger than a full-grown elephant! But it may not be very long before the

How does whaling affect the number of whales?

blue whale joins the dinosaur as a museum specimen, but no longer living. If this does happen, it will be due entirely to man's greed. It was not until the middle of the last century, when the harpoon gun was invented, that blue whales were hunted. Until then, only small whales were killed. But ever since, whales have been ruthlessly pursued.

The methods used to kill whales involve firing a harpoon filled with

explosives into the animal and then detonating the explosives. Although the methods used to kill whales are quicker than those used in the past, they would be considered outrageously cruel if they were used on any other animal. Whales are considered to be among the most intelligent of all mammals.

Several species of whales have already been completely exterminated or made very rare in the Atlantic by whaling, and elsewhere practically all the larger whales are being over-hunted. Restrictions on the numbers of whales that can be killed each year have been made — but sometimes the whaling fleets have been unable to catch even the few they were allowed to catch because the whales are getting so rare now. It is very likely that unless some species, such as the blue whale, are protected, they will soon become extinct.

TIGER

The trade in furs for women's coats has made the big cats rare.

Where can tigers still be found in the wild? There are relatively few places now where tigers can be found in the wild, although earlier this century there were places where they were still fairly abundant. They once were widespread in places as far apart as Persia, Java, Siberia, India, and China. Now they remain in only a few reserves and remote mountains. In Siberia and other parts of the U.S.S.R., tigers are strictly protected. In India and most other parts of their range they are given some sort of protection, but it is often very difficult to enforce the law. Fortunately, some tigers are being bred in zoos; but their future will be ensured only when really large tracts of suitable country, containing plenty of suitable animals for the tigers to feed upon, can be set aside.

On the island of Java there are probably no more than a dozen or so tigers left; about fifteen or twenty in Iran; some in Afghanistan. There are very

OCELOT

JAGUAR

SNOW LEOPARD

CHEETAH

few surviving in China, as they lived in fairly densely populated areas, and unlike most rare animals found in China, they are not protected. Tigers are protected in many parts of India, but although they are now very rare almost everywhere, tiger-hunting "shikars" are still advertised by some travel firms.

In the past, tigers, along with most other large predatory animals, have been accused of causing widespread damage to domestic animals and also of killing humans. But they usually take human life only when they are injured and unable to catch their normal food. Today there are too few of them left to be considered a serious menace to human life, but they are still hunted to make fur coats or rugs. A number of film stars and other well-known personalities have given up this fashion, emphasizing the fact that it was helping to make tigers and "spotted" cats (cheetahs, ocelots, and snow leopards) extinct. By wearing nylon fur, people can help save wild animals.

Britain is too far north for most species

What reptiles and amphibians are becoming extinct in Britain?

of reptiles and amphibians. Cold-blooded animals prefer a warmer climate. Of the few species found in the British Isles, three are in immediate danger of extinction: the sand lizard, the smooth snake, and the natterjack toad. Although they have probably never been numerous, the natterjack and sand lizard were once considerably more widespread. They have been declining for many years and now their extinction seems almost certain. All three species are found in sandy habitats, often near the coast. The main cause of their decline is habitat destruction. Fires are a danger — many sandy areas have gorse and heather which easily catch fire from a careless match or cigarette.

SMOOTH SNAKE

SAND LIZARD

NATTERJACK TOAD

DARTFORD WARBLER

Destruction of habitat endangers animals. As the heathlands are destroyed, so are the sand lizards, smooth snakes, natterjack toads, and Dartford warblers.

The Dartford warbler is a pretty, long-

Are heathland birds in danger?

tailed, pinkish bird that was often found in gorse and heather, but it has also become nearly extinct in Britain. This bird needs the gorse and heather to breed in, and it also needs mild winters. Every time there is a long, cold winter, many Dartford warblers die. The number left is now so small that it can be only a few years before they die out.

RARE AND EXTINCT BRITISH BIRDS

GREAT GRAY SHRIKE

OSPREY

KITE

WRYNECK

AVOCET

BLUE WHALE

SEA OTTER

KOMODO DRAGON

ORANGUTAN

NILE CROCODILE

SEYCHELLES FODY

GALAPAGOS TORTOISE

ASIAN LION

REENE'S PHEASANT

41

Père David's deer escaped from the Imperial Hunting Park and were killed by starving peasants.

Not only is the story of the survival of this deer interesting, but it is also one of the strangest looking deer. Père David's deer died out in the wild about three thousand years ago, when the swamps in which it lived in China were drained and farmed. For the next three thousand years it survived only in parks. In 1865, the French missionary and naturalist, Abbé Armand David, managed to peek over the walls of Non Hai-tzu — the Imperial Hunting Park in Peking — and saw the last remaining herd of these deer. During the next year Père David managed to get hold of two skins which he sent to the Paris Natural History Museum, and the new species was named after him. A little later several live deer were sent to zoos in Europe. Then, in 1894, during a famine, a flood burst through the walls of the Hunting Park and most of the deer escaped, only to be killed

What is Père David's deer?

The Duke of Bedford's herd of Père David's deer preserved the species from extinction.

and eaten by the starving peasants. Those that managed to survive were killed by foreign soldiers during the Boxer Rebellion in 1900. By 1911 there were only two left in China.

Realizing that Père David's deer was about to become extinct, the Duke of Bedford, a zoologist, gathered together all the animals he could. He collected them from zoos and parks throughout Europe, and formed a herd on his estate at Woburn. They started breeding, and by 1922, just after the last two had died in China, he had over 60. After the Second World War, surplus animals were sent from Woburn to other zoos, and by the early 1960's there were altogether over 400. Then, in 1964, London Zoo sent four animals to Peking. Thus, Père David's deer became one of the first animals to be saved from almost certain extinction by breeding in captivity. It emphasized the important work that zoos can do for conservation.

Is the human race becoming extinct?

Man is, of course, an animal, and at the present time is increasing very rapidly — so rapidly, in fact, that he is spreading into all corners of the world and often causing other species of animals to become extinct.

Several races of humans have become extinct. When Charles Darwin visited Tierra del Fuego, at the southernmost tip of South America, in 1832, there were about three thousand Yahgans. They lived in one of the bleakest parts of the world in a very primitive state — they were extremely tough and hunted and slept almost naked in the snow and rain. But although they could survive the hardships of climate, they could not fight off the diseases Europeans brought with them. Also, the clothing well-meaning missionaries and settlers gave them merely kept them wet. When they wore no clothes, they quickly dried. Typhoid, measles, TB, pneumonia and flu killed them off, and by 1933 there were only about 40 Yahgans left. Now they have all died, and what was once a

The Yahgans could resist terrible weather—but not European diseases.

44

European settlers hunted Tasmanians as if they were wild animals. They were all extinct by 1876.

flourishing tribe is known only by drawings, photographs, and the things they made.

The story of the Tasmanians is a shocking one. When Captain James Cook visited Tasmania (or Van Diemen's Land, as it was then known), he described the Tasmanian aborigines as being mild and cheerful. In 1798, the first European settlers arrived and a prison colony of convicts sent from England was set up. The Tasmanians were still living in the Stone Age and could not understand the new ways. When they saw cattle and sheep instead of kangaroos, they hunted them. The Tasmanians were hunted as if they were animals, and by 1835 there were only about two hundred of them left. A missionary named George Robinson persuaded them to go to Flinders Island, where they would be protected, but tribal life was discontinued. The last Tasmanian aborigine died in 1876.

Europeans took the Red Indians' lands away from them—often by force.

Has man exterminated other men anywhere else in the world?

In many parts of the world, man has tried to get rid of other men. During the last century, when empires were being expanded, settlers left Europe for far-flung parts of the world. Many of these places were already inhabited, and if the native population could not be enslaved, they were often driven out or killed. In the New World the white men drove Indians from their tribal hunting grounds, and when the Indians fought back, the white men declared war and tried to exterminate them.

When Captain Cook went to New Zealand, there were about 10,000 Maoris living there. When the white settlers arrived, they fought the terrible

In the Xingu National Park the Brazilian Indians

At one time the plains of Argentina were inhabited by Indians. Now gauchos herd cattle where Indians were massacred.

Maori Wars. By 1896, there were 42,-000 Maoris, but the settlers had increased to about 500,000.

The South American Indians have suffered particularly badly at the hands of the white men. They have been driven out of the plains of Argentina, where gauchos now raise cattle. In Brazil, about a hundred tribes are known to have been exterminated since 1500. The persecution and extermination still continues. Simply meeting a white man can be fatal to the primitive tribes living in remote jungles of the Amazon basin, because they have no way of fighting off diseases such as the common cold. In an attempt to halt the exploitation of lands where Indians live and to protect them from disease, the government of Brazil created Xingu

0 square miles which are protected from exploitation.

National Park in 1962. This park consists of about 8,500 square miles of the tribal lands of the Xingu peoples — who in 1884 were thought to have a population of about three thousand, but by 1962 had been reduced to only three hundred.

Many scientists also believe that man may be destroying himself by over-populating the world — there just is not enough food to feed everyone now, let alone in the future. Unless the numbers of humans are controlled, famines, plagues, and wars will become more common — they are nature's way of restoring a balance.

Since 1900 roughly one species has become extinct every year. They are being pushed out by man. Unless man stops spreading, there will soon be no room left for wild animals..